Trouble on the Farm

How Farmers Meet the Challenges of Nature

Daniel Ahearn

Contents

Rigby

A Harcourt Achieve Imprint

www.Rigby.com
1-800-531-5015

Why Prices Go Up and Down

Have you ever heard your parents complain about the rising prices of food while shopping at the supermarket? Why do these prices change? Who sets food prices in the first place, farmers or store owners?

Usually, if there is a big harvest of a crop, creating a big **supply**, prices for that kind of food tend to go down. But if something happens to the crop and there is a **shortage**, prices tend to rise.

Many different things affect the prices we pay for food.

APPLES

$1.39

When farmers bring in a large harvest, there is so much food that they have to offer the food to suppliers at a lower price. No farmer wants to get stuck with an unsold crop. The suppliers will probably lower their prices to sell their food to stores more quickly. Stores lower their own prices, hoping to sell more because they're giving good prices to people who shop with them. In this way, families just like yours hope to save money on food.

Of course, the opposite is also true—if the farmers' harvests are small, the price of food will go up.

Prices can also change because of changing **demand**. For example, in the days leading up to Thanksgiving, many people want turkeys. If there are more customers than the stores and the farmers are prepared for, the price of turkeys may rise. The suppliers of turkeys, however, expect the increased demand around Thanksgiving. They try to have plenty of turkeys on hand for people to buy.

Again, the opposite can be true. During the rest of the year, when only a few people want turkey for dinner, you are able to buy a turkey for less money.

Changing demand can make the price of food go up or down.

To explain why the amount of available food changes, we have to go to the farms where the fruits, vegetables, grains, and **livestock** are grown. Crops need good weather, sunlight, and rainfall in just the right amounts. Too much or too little of any of these things can mean a small harvest and a small supply. Hurricanes, hail, ice storms, insects, and plant and animal diseases can really make a difference in the amount of food farmers grow. All of these things affect what we will pay for that food at the store.

Farming is hard work. Farmers are awake before the sun rises and are on the go until after sundown. It is a risky business, because farmers depend on good weather to make their crops grow. And no one can say what the weather will be like for more than a few days at a time.

The wrong kind of weather can hurt a farmer's chances of bringing in a good harvest.

Keeping crops free of insects and disease is expensive for farmers.

Farmers constantly battle against the forces of nature to grow the food we eat. Farmers have to make sure there will be enough water to keep crops and livestock alive. Sometimes they have to add **fertilizers**, or chemical plant food, to the soil to feed their crops. They often use other chemicals called **pesticides** to protect their crops and livestock from insects and disease. Fertilizers and pesticides are expensive, and the cost is passed along to suppliers, stores, and then to your family when you and your family buy food at the supermarket.

Let's take a closer look at some of the problems farmers have to face and how this affects the price of food.

Frost

Do you enjoy a glass of sweet orange juice at breakfast or for a snack later in the day? Many people around the world love orange juice. The demand for oranges is always high, so farmers can make a lot of money growing oranges and other **citrus** fruits.

What challenges do farmers face when they grow oranges and other citrus fruits? Like most plants, oranges need water, sunlight, and warm weather to grow. But oranges don't do well in cold weather at all. Even in usually warm states such as Florida, California, and Texas, the three most important citrus-growing states, temperatures in orange groves can sometimes fall below freezing. If oranges freeze, they are ruined and cannot be sold. If an orange tree freezes, the tree may die. If many trees are affected, it can mean a huge loss of money for the orange grower.

Most oranges used for juice come from Florida, while most oranges for eating, like these, come from California.

In the 1980s, Florida suffered several frosts, or periods of freezing weather. These frosts seriously damaged the orange crop and cost the farmers a lot of money. As a result, the farmers had to come up with better ways to make sure the temperature in the orange groves stayed above freezing during periods of frost. One old way was to use large, smoky heaters called smudge pots to warm the air around the orange trees during a frost.

Smudge pot heaters such as these are seldom used in orange groves today.

Surprisingly, covering orange trees with ice can save both the trees and the oranges from the damaging effects of frost.

Though smudge pots helped warm the air, they also created a lot of air pollution. So orange growers began to fight frosts with wind machines, which they placed on towers. These machines look like giant fans. Although fans are usually used to keep things cool, these fans mix the warmer air high above the orange trees with colder air closer to the ground. The wind machines can keep the temperature in the orange groves just above freezing.

Another way orange growers fight frosts may sound even stranger than using fans. Sometimes when temperatures are really cold, orange growers spray their trees and fruit with water, which covers everything in a thin coat of ice. The ice protects the oranges and trees from cold winds that might force temperatures even lower and destroy the crop.

No Rain

Like all living things, crops and livestock need water in order to live, so regular rainfall is important to farmers. Farmers need rain to soak the soil from time to time, because almost all plants absorb water through their roots. And rain fills lakes and ponds so farm animals can drink.

When there is little rainfall over a long period of time, it is called a **drought**. A drought is every farmer's nightmare. A drought means that there is not enough water in the soil for crops to grow. It can mean that livestock cannot find enough water to drink. If a drought lasts long enough, entire crops and herds of animals can die, forcing food prices to rise.

A drought also keeps grass from growing, so livestock have to be fed with hay. Sooner or later, hay runs out. Then farmers have to buy hay and other kinds of food for the livestock, and another cost gets passed on to suppliers, stores, and customers.

Droughts can sometimes be so bad that water supplies in **reservoirs** begin to run out. If a drought goes on long enough, cities and counties often have to limit the amount of water people and businesses use.

Almost nothing can grow in this dry soil. Drought is one of the worst things that can happen for a farmer.

Sometimes crop failure from drought can lead to even bigger problems. This was the case during the worst drought in American history. In 1931 much of the United States began to receive less rainfall than usual. By 1934 over 80 percent of the country—more than 30 states—was suffering from a lack of rainfall. Dry conditions continued for almost ten years, with drought records being set in 1936, 1939, and 1940.

For 50 years in the Great Plains region, farmers had been plowing up the grassland and planting crops. The roots of the natural plains grasses had always held the soil in place. But the new farm crops like wheat and cotton weren't planted as closely together as the grass. When the area was hit by drought, the result was a disaster.

In the 1930s, a large part of the country was as dry as dust. Storms could blow tons of dry soil for hundreds of miles.

NEBRASKA

COLORADO

DUST BOWL

KANSAS

NEW MEXICO

OKLAHOMA

TEXAS

The soil became so dry that the wind blew it away in enormous dust storms. The roots of the dead and dying farm plants couldn't hold the soil. The wind created dust clouds up to 1,500 miles long and 900 miles wide. Each year in the 1930s, there were more and more dust storms, including 38 in 1933 alone.

People of the Great Plains remember April 14, 1935, as Black Sunday. On that day, the worst dust storm yet blew across the plains destroying millions of acres of farmland. A large area of the Great Plains, including parts of Kansas, Nebraska, Colorado, Oklahoma, New Mexico, and Texas, came to be called the Dust Bowl.

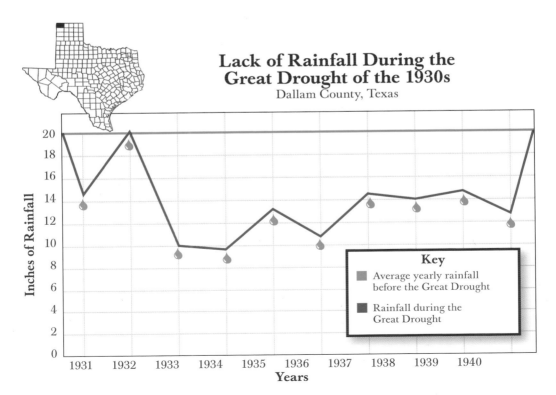

Lack of Rainfall During the Great Drought of the 1930s
Dallam County, Texas

Inches of Rainfall

Key
- Average yearly rainfall before the Great Drought
- Rainfall during the Great Drought

Years

Guarding Against Drought

The Great Drought of the 1930s was not the last drought to affect U.S. farmers by any means. Extremely dry conditions continue to happen from time to time. How do farmers fight this ongoing problem?

Irrigation is the replacement of rainfall with water from another source, such as a lake, a river, or a well. Sometimes people build dams across rivers and store water in reservoirs. The water may be moved directly to the fields or saved for use when there is little rainfall. Irrigation may be a farmer's only choice when the rain doesn't fall.

To make sure their crops are never too thirsty, farmers have invented many ways to irrigate their fields. The simplest way is to flood the fields. Suppose a farmer had a wheat field that was hit with a drought. If there were a river nearby, the farmer could dig a ditch and guide the water from the river to the field. Once the water reached the field, smaller ditches could be dug in the soil to bring water to each part of the field.

Farmers sometimes flood their fields to irrigate them.

One important source of water for irrigation is an aquifer. Aquifers are like underground lakes. Spaces in underground rocks sometimes hold lots of water. Farmers use pumps to bring underground water to the surface of the soil to irrigate their fields.

Farmers have to be careful about using the pumps too much. Modern pumps work so well that they can completely drain an aquifer before it has a chance to refill. This can lead to permanently empty aquifers or to water containing too many minerals, which can damage crops or make livestock sick.

Overhead sprinklers like these are commonly used to water farm crops. Water is sometimes pumped to the surface from deep underground.

The dripper is an irrigation method that delivers more water to the roots of the plant. Drip irrigation loses much less water to evaporation than do sprinklers.

Farmers sometimes use sprinklers to spread water on their crops. These work just like the sprinklers used to water lawns. One problem with overhead sprinklers is that some water is lost to evaporation. And high winds sometimes blow the water away before it can get to the roots of the plants.

One solution has been to put together long pipes on wheels with sprinklers mounted close to the ground. Electric motors move the pipes across the fields so that every plant gets water. Another method uses pipes laid on the ground. The pipes have holes on the bottom that slowly drip water onto the soil near the plants.

Pests

One of the greatest threats to the food supply comes from insects. An individual insect may be small, but a swarm of millions of insects can quickly destroy a wheat or corn crop. The locust, a kind of grasshopper, is one insect that can cause a lot of damage for farmers. One ton of locusts can eat as much food in one day as 2,500 human beings.

Locusts and other kinds of insects are greatly feared as pests, and they cause billions of dollars of damage to crops all over the world. In 2004 a huge swarm of desert locusts destroyed large amounts of the grain harvest in northern and western Africa, causing a terrible food shortage.

Wheat, corn, soybeans, and other important human food crops naturally draw a variety of insects looking for a free meal. Some insects, though, like the boll weevil, go after specific kinds of crops.

Cotton is a very important and valuable crop used mostly to make clothing. The boll weevil, which attacks and destroys cotton plants, first arrived in the United States around 1892. The boll weevil pierces a cotton plant with its snout. It then eats the tender young cotton fibers in the boll, or the fruit part of the plant. The weevil lays its eggs in holes in the cotton bolls so newly hatched young weevils will have plenty to eat. The boll weevil is still the greatest insect threat to cotton crops in the United States.

A farmer in western Africa walks in his fields after they were destroyed by locusts. Pests such as locusts can cause great damage to crops.

For a century, scientists and farmers have tried to destroy the boll weevil, but the insect keeps coming back. In 1996 cotton farmers in Virginia found the boll weevil attacking their crops once again. Farmers applied tons of pesticides to their crops to control the destructive insects.

Pesticides kill bugs, but sometimes they can also be dangerous to humans and other animals. Plants absorb some chemical pesticides, and others are washed by rain into rivers and lakes. Humans and animals can take in pesticides when they eat **contaminated** food or drink contaminated water. Some insects develop resistance to certain pesticides so that they no longer work.

Pesticides help protect crops from pests such as the boll weevil, but they can sometimes be harmful to animals and people.

Before scientists realized that DDT could be very harmful to humans and animals, people used the chemical to control mosquitoes as well as farm pests.

One of the first modern pesticides was DDT. DDT was useful for killing insects, but it also produced harmful effects on the environment. DDT was not easily washed away by water, and it remained in the environment for a long time. It also collected in the bodies of animals and humans. Scientists discovered that DDT made birds lay eggs with shells that were too thin. The eggs broke easily, and the baby birds died. So many young birds died that the survival of some kinds of birds, including pelicans, peregrine falcons, and bald eagles, was threatened. When the bald eagle was placed on the endangered list in 1972, people stopped using DDT. However, many other chemicals have taken its place.

Going Organic

Some farmers are trying to fight harmful insects and diseases without the use of chemicals. They do so by introducing useful insects into their fields. These insects are the natural predators of the crop-destroying pests. For example, a wasp called the trichogramma eats the eggs of two damaging insects, the corn borer and the cabbage looper. Trichogramma is not harmful to other animals, humans, or crops. This kind of farming is called **organic** farming. Organic farming uses no man-made chemicals.

Scientists are working on ways to use tiny worm-like animals called nematodes, which live deep in the soil, to replace pesticides. Some kinds of nematodes attack plants, but others attack the insects that feed on crops. The "good" nematodes kill the insects and multiply inside the dead bugs. Then the young nematodes go on to destroy other crop-damaging insects. Scientists and farmers who are working on the experiment are careful to use only those nematodes that don't like to eat the crop they are trying to protect.

Scientists hope that worm-like nematodes will help protect organic farms from harmful insects.

Crop Disease

A crop disease is just like a disease in humans or animals. Crop diseases can damage or even kill a farmer's crop. The signs of crop diseases are often easy to see. A plant's leaves might turn yellow or **wilt**. The plant might grow strangely, with patches, lumps, or knots instead of its normal appearance. Diseased crops might not grow to their full size.

Plant diseases can sometimes be caused by pollution in the air or water. But germs or funguses usually cause the most dangerous crop diseases. Sometimes insects that aren't harmful to crops carry germs that *are* harmful. And sometimes, creatures such as nematodes, which scientists use to protect some kinds of crops, will attack and destroy other kinds of crops.

Corn smut is a crop disease caused by funguses.

Natural Disasters

When people think of natural disasters, they usually picture huge, violent events like hurricanes, tornadoes, and earthquakes. Natural disasters cannot be prevented, and most are almost impossible to predict. Different kinds of natural disasters can affect farm crops and the food supply in different ways.

Floods

The damage that floods cause to crops and livestock depends on things like how deep the flood waters are, the amount of time the fields are under water, and the temperature of the water.

Plants take in air just like animals, so they can drown when they are under water. Warm water carries less oxygen than cold water, so more crop damage is usually caused by floods in late spring when water is warmer. Long after the floodwaters have gone away, the soil may still be soaked with water, preventing crop roots from getting the oxygen they need.

Not all livestock can swim, so floods present a huge danger to farm animals. Usually, livestock must be rescued and moved to high, dry ground in order to survive a flood.

In 1993 the Mississippi and Missouri rivers flooded. Floodwaters covered the ground for more than two months, causing huge damage to crops and destroying livestock.

Hurricanes

In 1938 a strong hurricane struck New England without warning. Besides damage caused to cities and towns, farmers lost fruit trees and potato crops. The United States government estimated that millions of trees were blown down in New England at a loss of about 150 million dollars.

Orange growers in Florida face dangers from hurricanes almost every year. Most of the crop damage from hurricanes comes from high winds and flooding. In 2004 3 hurricanes in a 6-week period damaged the Florida orange crop even worse than the repeated frosts of the 1980s.

In 2004, Hurricane Charley destroyed one third of the orange groves in Florida. The entire citrus industry lost hundreds of millions of dollars.

Hurricane Strength

Strength	Wind	Effects	
1	Strongest gusts less than 77 miles per hour	Damage to some crops, trees and mobile homes	4–5 foot waves
2	Strongest gusts 77 to 106 miles per hour	Minor house damages Damage to small boats Heavy crop damage	6–8 foot waves
3	Strongest gusts 106 to 140 miles per hour	Some roof and structural damage; power failure likely	9–12 foot waves
4	Strongest gusts 140 to 175 miles per hour	Significant structural damage Widespread power failure Dangerous flying wreckage	13–18 foot waves
5	Strongest gusts above 175 miles per hour	Major damage	over 18 foot waves

The 2004 hurricanes also did great damage to cotton, peanuts, and pecans, with North Carolina alone claiming 50 million dollars in crop losses. Cotton farmers reported that 100-mile-per-hour winds completely stripped ripe cotton plants of their blossoms.

Scientists also think that hurricanes brought a plant disease called soybean rust to the United States. The first time this disease was seen in North America was in 2004 after the hurricanes hit.

Hail

Hail storms drop pellets of ice that form inside rain clouds. Hailstones can range from the size of a pea to the size of a softball. These falling chunks of ice can do millions of dollars of damage to crops every year. Imagine pieces of ice the size of golf balls or baseballs falling onto a field of young corn or soybeans. The crops could take quite a beating.

Wheat and soybeans may be broken or crushed by the falling hailstones. Grain can actually be knocked loose from the plant stems. Hailstones can strip the leaves from corn, sunflowers, and fruit trees, slowing growth or destroying the crop. Sometimes a whole crop may have to be re-planted for the farmer to make any money at all—and these extra costs show up in higher food prices.

Fortunately, hailstorms are rare, and many farmers buy crop **insurance** to protect themselves from losing too much money.

Large hailstones can cause severe crop damage.

Wildfires threaten lives as well as farmland.

Wildfires

Wildfires are ground or forest fires that have gotten out of control. Human beings accidentally start many wildfires, but many start during thunderstorms from lightning strikes. More than 100,000 wildfires break out every year in the United States, and they destroy millions of acres of woods, fields, and grassland.

Trees are valuable to farmers for the fruit and nuts they produce, but trees also provide construction material, paper, and many other products. When trees are destroyed by fires or other natural disasters, the price of wood rises, but so do the costs of newspapers, napkins, stationary—all the paper products we use every day. The loss of trees causes lumber prices to rise rapidly. Trees take a long time to grow, so the high prices can remain for years.

Indoor Farming

Outdoor farming can be very risky. In order to try to control some of the conditions in which their crops grow, some farmers build greenhouses. A greenhouse—sometimes called a hothouse—is a shelter for crops. Greenhouses are made of glass or plastic, and they allow the sun's rays through to warm the plants and soil. The glass roof and walls keep heat from escaping, so the greenhouse stays warm. Sometimes other materials, such as tubs of water, gravel, or sand, are added to the inside of the greenhouse because they absorb heat to keep the greenhouse warm at night.

Greenhouses are used to grow warm-weather vegetables, flowers, and fruit all year long. For example, tomatoes are a summer crop, but the tomatoes you ate last winter were probably grown in a greenhouse.

Because greenhouse crops are sheltered from the weather, they must be irrigated to supply them with water. Pests and diseases must also be kept out, because in a closed building they could quickly destroy a crop.

Greenhouses can protect crops from cold weather, insects, disease, and drought.

An outdoor farmer needs the sun's light and heat and nature's rainfall to help his crops grow. Outdoor farmers don't have to pay for sunshine or rain. Greenhouse farming is much more expensive because of the extra cost of building and maintaining the greenhouse and providing the man-made environment. The prices of the greenhouse crops are usually much higher. But many customers are willing to pay the higher prices to have fresh vegetables or flowers in the middle of a long, cold winter.

Hydroponics is farming without soil. Soil normally stores the **nutrients** that plants need in order to grow. If nutrients are fed to the plants directly through the water, then soil is not necessary for the crop to grow.

Many types of flowers are grown year-round in greenhouses.

A large hydroponic crop

Hydroponic crops are usually planted in clay pebbles, sand, or some other similar material that will hold the plants up and allow plenty of oxygen to get to the roots. In the simplest hydroponic farms, the crops are planted in trays that are set into containers of water and nutrients. Another method is to flood the plant's roots with nutrients and water and allow them to drain slowly. Hydroponic greenhouse gardens are used in Antarctica to supply scientists and researchers with fresh vegetables in the cold climate. Large hydroponic farms can be complicated, and computers are used to control things like light, nutrient supply, and temperature. These controls make hydroponics the most expensive way to farm. If hydroponic farming is done correctly, however, the controlled conditions produce greater harvests than ordinary outdoor farming.

Farming in the Future

Farmers always want to take the risk out of raising crops. Greenhouses equipped with hydroponic equipment and controlled by computers may be the future of farming. Computers could control heat, light, water, and nutrients to produce large harvests again and again. The only thing holding these new methods back is the high cost of energy for heat and light. If these problems are solved, who knows what farmers might accomplish?

Is this the shape of the future? Japanese farmers grew these square watermelons inside glass containers. Square watermelons will be easier to ship, and they'll fit in your refrigerator better!

No one knows for sure how much oranges, apples, tomatoes, or corn might cost at the store a year from now. Prices will depend on whether farmers win their battles with drought, wind, frost, pests, and natural disasters. If the farmers are lucky and there is rain and sunshine in just the right amounts, the crops can be harvested and sold at fair prices.

The next time you go shopping for groceries with your parents, look at the prices. If you hear your parents speak about the high price of fruit, vegetables, or paper products, you'll understand some of the many reasons why.

Prices for farm products will always change from year to year.

Glossary

citrus fruits like oranges, grapefruits, lemons, and limes

contaminated containing something bad or unhealthy

demand how much people want something

fertilizers food for crops placed in the soil by farmers

insurance protection against loss of something, such as property

irrigation the placemet of rainfsll with water from another source.

livestock farm animals, such as horses, cows, sheep, and chickens.

nutrients the things plants or animals need to survive

organic–natural, or without the use of chemicals

pesticides chemicals used to control insects and disease

reservoirs -made lakes used to store water

shortage not enough of something

supply the amount of something available to be bought

wilt dry or shrink up

Index